WELLINGTON SQUARE

Drea

Christine Butterw

Contents

We all dream

Do you dream?

We all dream when we sleep, but we don't always remember our dreams.

People have different sorts of sleep
in one night.

We all dream four or five times in one night.

We start the night with a deep sleep just after we go to bed.

Then we have our first dream.

After, we have more deep sleep.

Then we have a second dream.

We have a light sleep near morning.

Then comes our third dream.

Our last bit of sleep is not so deep.

Our last dream comes just before we wake. If we wake while we are dreaming, we will remember the dream.

Why do we dream?

Why do you dream?

A dream may be a way to think about what we did in the day.

We may dream of things we wish could happen.

We may dream about things that scare us.

We may dream about things that we wish we could have.

A dream may show us the answer to a problem we can't solve.

Our brain finds the answer while we sleep.

Daydreaming

Sometimes, when we are awake, we think about something so much we don't notice what is going on around us. We call this daydreaming.

What do you daydream about?

Odd facts about dreams

- When we dream, we still know about things that happen around us.

- We often make these things into part of our dream.

- We may feel something and put that in the dream.

- We may hear a noise and put that in the dream.

- Even when you are fast asleep, you know your dream isn't real.

Do animals dream?

Animals seem to dream too.

A cat or dog moves its eyes as it sleeps,
just like we do.

It may move its eyes or nose, or its paws may twitch. It seems to be dreaming about its daytime life.

Elephants, horses and even some birds seem to dream.

Animals may have funny dreams like these, but we may never know!

Glossary

daydream – to dream while awake

dream – to imagine things are happening while asleep

fact – something that is true

odd – strange

sleep – to rest completely with closed eyes

solve – to find the answer to a problem or mystery

scare – frighten

twitch – move very quickly